Soul Retreats

_____

Presented To

_____

Presented By

_____

Date

Soul Retreats™ for Couples
ISBN 0-310-80186-9

Copyright 2003 by GRQ Ink, Inc.
Franklin, Tennessee 37067
"Soul Retreats" is a trademark owned by GRQ, Inc.

Published by Inspirio™, The gift group of Zondervan
5300 Patterson Avenue, SE
Grand Rapids, Michigan 49530

Requests for information should be addressed to:
Inspirio™, The gift group of Zondervan
Grand Rapids, Michigan 49530

http://www.inspiriogifts.com

Editor and Compiler: Lila Empson
Associate Editor: Janice Jacobson
Project Manager: Tom Dean
Manuscript written by Moira Allaby in conjunction with Snapdragon Editorial Group, Inc.
Design: Whisner Design Group

Soul Retreats
for Couples

inspirio™

Contents

Introduction

Finding time for each other—time for your souls to grow close, time for each to learn the other's ways, time for your souls to discover the wonder of living together under God's care. This special time is important for every relationship. But time alone is often elusive, swallowed up in the minutia of everyday life.

Soul Retreats™ *for Couples* is designed especially for people like you who want to share precious moments in the midst of your busy lives. These thirty retreats offer ideas to replenish your inner resources through such activities as music, literature, gardening, and prayer.

Browse through the retreat titles each day and choose the selection that interests you, or simply read the retreats in the order they appear. Either way, you will discover encouragement, strength, and insight directed specifically to you as a couple.

I My Best– Beloved's Am

Even like two little bank-dividing brooks,

That wash the pebbles with their wanton streams,

And having ranged and searched a thousand nooks,

Meet both at length in silver-breasted Thames,

Where in a greater current they conjoin:

So I my best-beloved's am; so he is mine.

Francis Quarles

Stargazing

Set aside some time for gazing at the stars with your spouse. Stargazing has always been a popular activity, especially for couples. Staring up at the expanse of blackness and the bright pinpoints of light surrounding the creamy whiteness of the moon inspires the soul. The frustrations and cares of life seem small and manageable when compared to the greatness of God's creation.

On the next clear evening, throw a blanket on the ground or place a couple of lawn chairs side by side. Find a spot where you can be away from porch lights and streetlights. Spread out, sit back, and get comfortable. Then look up into the heavens and let your souls bask in the magnificent light show.

As you take in the view, consider that God, who made all that lies before you, lovingly and carefully crafted each one of you as well. In the Bible, he reveals that his human creations are the capstone of all he made. And imagine this: Everything you love and admire in each other was first a creative thought in the mind of God.

Take hands as you gaze upward and whisper a few words of thanks for all the beauty God has created in the heavens.

*Be glad of life because it gives you the chance
to love and to work and to play and to look
up at the stars.*
—HENRY VAN DYKE

A Moment to Reflect

One of the greatest benefits of gazing up at the starry sky is that you can better appreciate how truly great God is. If he is great enough to create the great expanse of space—the sun, the moon, the sparkling stars, and the glowing planets—then surely he is great enough to take care of the things that concern the two of you, his dearest creation.

Find time to sit together under the stars. Let your minds marvel at what lies before your eyes. Take it all in and let it lift and refresh your souls.

The spacious firmament on high,
With all the blue ethereal sky,
And spangled heavens,
A shining frame.
Their great Original proclaim.
Forever singing, as they shine,
The hand that made us is divine.

—JOSEPH ADDISON

By the word of the LORD were the heavens made, their starry host by the breath of his mouth.

Psalm 33:6 NIV

A Moment to Refresh

God made two great lights—the greater light to govern the day and the lesser light to govern the night. He also made the stars. God set them in the expanse of the sky to give light on the earth.

Genesis 1:16–17 NIV

Give thanks to the LORD, for he is good. His love endures forever . . . Who by his understanding made the heavens . . . the moon and stars to govern the night; His love endures forever.

Psalm 136:1, 5, 9 NIV

You alone are the LORD. You made the heavens, even the highest heavens, and all their starry host, the earth and all that is on it, the seas and all that is in them. You give life to everything, and the multitudes of heaven worship you.

Nehemiah 9:6 NIV

A world above man's head, to let him see how boundless might his soul's horizon be.

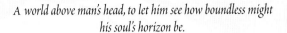

—Matthew Arnold

He determines the number of the stars and calls them each by name. Great is our Lord and mighty in power; his understanding has no limit.

Psalm 147:4–5 NIV

Lift your eyes and look to the heavens: Who created all these? He who brings out the starry host one by one, and calls them each by name. Because of his great power and mighty strength, not one of them is missing.

Isaiah 40:26 NIV

The LORD said, "It is I who made the earth and created mankind upon it. My own hands stretched out the heavens; I marshaled their starry hosts."

Isaiah 45:12 NIV

Everywhere I find the signature, the autograph of God.

—Joseph Parker

On Your Knees

A Moment to Pause Choose a place to pray where you can sit close together. If possible, hold hands. The best time to pray together depends completely on your own schedules and comfort level. You may want to pray as soon as you wake up in the morning or right before you go to sleep at night. Before meals or before you leave for the office are also good times.

Give yourself a few moments to relax and feel comfortable in God's presence. Then, take turns speaking to him as simply and honestly as you can. Tell him about the things you are facing in your lives—in as little or as much detail as you wish. Forget about using impressive words or conforming to formalities when you pray. Just speak to God from your hearts. He hears every word.

Prayer is a soul booster. Releasing your concerns to almighty God and talking things over with him can provide a significant level of peace, comfort, and perspective. Praying as a couple enhances the experience. It can make you each more sensitive to the other's personal needs and point of view, and motivate you to trust God for shared concerns.

Prayer is a rising up and a drawing near to God in mind, and in heart, and in spirit.
—ALEXANDER WHYTE

A Moment to Reflect

Prayer is a wonderful gift. It is a gift to be able to put all your cares and concerns into the hands of your loving heavenly father and receive his mercy, peace, and comfort in return. It is a gift to be able to share prayer with your spouse.

Take a retreat for your souls by praying together as often as you can. God is always listening. As the two of you receive the answers to your prayers, come together in prayer as a couple once again to thank God. God is working his miracles through you.

Prayer makes sour hearts sweet,
Sad hearts merry,
Poor hearts rich, Foolish hearts wise,
Timid hearts brave, Sick hearts well,
Blind hearts full of sight,
Cold hearts ardent.
It drives our hungry souls
up into the fullness of God.

—Mechthild of Magheburg

13

*Pray in the Spirit on all occasions with all
kinds of prayers and requests.*

Ephesians 6:18 NIV

A Moment to Refresh

*Jesus said, "I tell you that if two of you on earth
agree about anything you ask for, it will be done
for you by my Father in heaven. For where two
or three come together in my name, there am I
with them."*

Matthew 18:19–20 NIV

*Confess your sins to one another, and pray for
one another, so that you may be healed. The
prayer of the righteous is powerful and effective.*

James 5:16 NRSV

*Pray without ceasing; in everything give thanks;
for this is God's will for you in Christ Jesus.*

1 Thessalonians 5:17–18 NASB

*Beloved, build yourselves up on your most holy
faith; pray in the Holy Spirit.*

Jude 20 NRSV

Prayer is less about changing the world than it is about changing ourselves.

❧

—David J. Wolpe

I urge that supplications, prayers, intercessions, and thanksgivings be made for everyone, for kings and all who are in high positions, so that we may lead a quiet and peaceable life in all godliness and dignity.

1 Timothy 2:1–2 NRSV

This is the confidence we have in approaching God: that if we ask anything according to his will, he hears us. And if we know that he hears us—whatever we ask—we know that we have what we asked of him.

1 John 5:14–15 NIV

Jesus said, "Whatever you ask for in prayer, believe that you have received it, and it will be yours."

Mark 11:24 NIV

Every time we pray our horizon is altered, our attitude about things is altered, not sometimes but every time.

❧

—Oswald Chambers

Dreams for Two

Set aside some special time—a quiet dinner, a picnic in the country, a rendezvous on the porch swing.

Choose a place where you can be comfortable and avoid interruptions. And for a little while, put your current concerns on hold—problems with the children, home repairs, financial decisions, health issues. Relax and enjoy being together.

The dreams God has placed in your hearts are precious for they hold the promise of the future. Creating an opportunity to share those dreams with each other can be satisfying, inspiring you to identify common goals, bonding you together in your resolve, and urging you on to accomplish God's best purposes for your lives.

Dreams are small beginnings with vast possibilities. They have the potential to change your life. Take your time. Give yourselves an opportunity to really hear each other. With God behind your dreams, you have unlimited possibilities.

As you share your ideas, your passions, your plans, ask God to guide your thinking. Ask him to help you sort through the dreams you have unveiled and make clear which ones he has called you to fulfill. Then thank him for the opportunity to accomplish his purposes in his perfect time.

There are no rules of architecture for
a castle in the clouds.
—G. K. CHESTERTON

A Moment to Reflect

Talking about your dreams in safety and confidence is a wonderfully intimate way to share with your spouse. When you share your dreams with each other, you put words to what were once personal interior concepts, ideas, thoughts. Speaking your dreams aloud gives them definition and allows them the promise of fulfillment.

Finding hope for your future together is spiritually exhilarating; sharing your dreams encourages the two of you to link arms and walk together with greater boldness and resolve into the future. It's a wonderful way to keep your outlook refreshed and your relationship strong.

When the dream in our heart is one that God has planted there, a strange happiness flows into us. At that moment all of the spiritual resources of the universe are released to help us. Our praying is then at one with the will of God and becomes a channel for the Creator's always joyous, triumphant purposes for us and our world.

—CATHERINE WOOD MARSHALL

The path of the righteous is like the first gleam of dawn, shining ever brighter till the full light of day.

Proverbs 4:18 NIV

A Moment to Refresh

The LORD said, "I alone know the plans I have for you, plans to bring you prosperity and not disaster, plans to bring about the future you hope for."

Jeremiah 29:11 GNT

The LORD answered me and said: Write the vision; make it plain on tablets, so that a runner may read it. For there is still a vision for the appointed time; it speaks of the end, and does not lie, if it seems to tarry, wait for it; it will surely come, it will not delay.

Habakkuk 2:2–3 NRSV

Two are better than one because they have a good return for their labor. For if either of them falls, the one will lift up his companion.

Ecclesiastes 4:9–10 NASB

Vision is the art of seeing things invisible.

—JONATHAN SWIFT

People learn from one another, just as iron sharpens iron.

Proverbs 27:17 GNT

May he give you the desire of your heart and make all your plans succeed.

Psalm 20:4 NIV

Plans fail for lack of counsel, but with many advisers they succeed.

Proverbs 15:22 NIV

To him who is able to do immeasurably more than all we ask or imagine, according to his power that is at work within us, to him be glory in the church and in Christ Jesus throughout all generations, for ever and ever!

Ephesians 3:20–21 NIV

Dream the impossible dream. Dreaming it may make it possible. It often has.

—AUTHOR UNKNOWN

Side by Side

A Moment to Pause

Plan a walk today, perhaps in the early morning when the air is fresh and the sun is just beginning to make an appearance. It's fun to be together first thing before the demands of the day start. Evening is also a good time to walk, just before dusk, as the brilliant colors of the sunset decorate the sky. Take the opportunity to set aside the busyness of the day and reestablish the special rhythm of your life together as you walk.

Purposefully strolling along a quiet street, a wooded trail, or even a sandy beach can provide an opportunity for relaxed conversation, renew you mentally and spiritually, and give you healthy exercise.

As you walk, make a game of it. Notice your footsteps. Who walks faster? Whose steps are longer? Do your arms swing in unison? Do you hold hands? Listen to the rhythm of your breathing, separately and together. Notice how each of you responds to obstacles in the path. Think about how God caused your steps to cross and how he brought you together to pursue his purposes.

Most of all, enjoy the physical connectedness of walking side by side, being one unit, each of you complementing and fulfilling the other.

Everywhere is walking distance if you have the time.
—STEVEN WRIGHT

A Moment to Reflect

God sees you and loves each of you as individuals, and he loves you as a couple. Your walk with each other represents your commitment to love and support each other, your commitment to walk together through the ups and downs of life. At a word from you, God walks alongside.

God will teach you to walk in harmony with each other by giving you an appreciation for your differences and similarities, and he will provide you with wisdom and counsel as you come across obstacles in life's path that threaten to cause you to stumble.

Walk quietly—
And know that He is God.
Let your life be governed by His guiding hand
E'en though it varies from the way you planned,
Bow your head in sweet submission and
Walk quietly—

ॐ

—Author Unknown

21

If we walk in the light, as he is in the light, we have fellowship with one another.

1 John 1:7 NIV

A Moment to Refresh

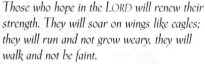

Those who hope in the LORD will renew their strength. They will soar on wings like eagles; they will run and not grow weary, they will walk and not be faint.

Isaiah 40:31 NIV

He who walks with the wise grows wise.

Proverbs 13:20 NIV

Physical exercise has some value, but spiritual exercise is valuable in every way, because it promises life both for the present and for the future.

1 Timothy 4:8 GNT

Give me understanding, and I will keep your law and obey it with all my heart. Direct me in the path of your commands, for there I find delight. Turn my heart toward your statutes and not toward selfish gain.

Psalm 119:34–36 NIV

Not to go back is somewhat to advance. And men must walk, at least, before they dance.

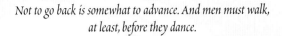

—ALEXANDER POPE

The LORD gives wisdom, and from his mouth come knowledge and understanding.
Proverbs 2:6 NIV

Blessed are those who have learned to acclaim you, who walk in the light of your presence, O LORD.
Psalm 89:15 NIV

Live in harmony with one another.
1 Peter 3:8 NIV

Walk in all the way that the LORD your God has commanded you.
Deuteronomy 5:33 NIV

Let your eyes look straight ahead, fix your gaze directly before you. Make level paths for your feet and take only ways that are firm. Do not swerve to the right or the left; keep your foot from evil.
Proverbs 4:25–27 NIV

What saves a man is to take a step. Then another step.

—ANTOINE DE SAINT-EXUPERY

Tell It Again

A Moment to Pause

Set aside an evening to watch a funny movie together or read a humorous book out loud. Consult a video guide together and then check out a comedy special at your local video rental store. Or look through your local library's books of humor (look under category 817 in the Dewey Decimal System).

Welcome laughter as a respected guest in your home. Put aside any work concerns or domestic quandaries. Break away from reality and indulge in the ridiculous. Smile. Let laughter and good humor ease any tension.

Surveys and studies repeatedly come up with this interesting fact: Couples who have been married for a long time often cite a healthy sense of humor as one of the keys to their marital success. Among other things, these couples report, humor has the ability to defuse an emotional situation, relieve stress, and keep lines of communication open.

God created you with an appreciation for the laughable and the ludicrous. Thank God for your ability to laugh—and make good use of it. And don't forget to thank him for this amazing gift that allows you to break away for a time from the grip of reality for your souls' sake.

A good laugh is sunshine in a house.
—WILLIAM MAKEPEACE THACKERY

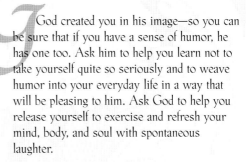

A Moment to Reflect

God created you in his image—so you can be sure that if you have a sense of humor, he has one too. Ask him to help you learn not to take yourself quite so seriously and to weave humor into your everyday life in a way that will be pleasing to him. Ask God to help you release yourself to exercise and refresh your mind, body, and soul with spontaneous laughter.

Consider how many ways and under which circumstances you can use your sense of humor to keep the atmosphere light in your home and in your relationship.

Everything's quiet,
except what's inside.
It's gurgling, threatening
to burst open wide.
I struggle to conquer the tickle within
But the laugh I've tried stifling
eventually wins.

✣

—CATHERINE ATKINSON

25

The joy of the LORD is your strength.
Nehemiah 8:10 NIV

A Moment to Refresh

The LORD your God is with you, he is mighty to save. He will take great delight in you, he will quiet you with his love, he will rejoice over you with singing.
Zephaniah 3:17 NIV

To the man who pleases him, God gives wisdom, knowledge and happiness.
Ecclesiastes 2:26 NIV

Weeping may last for the night, but a shout of joy comes in the morning.
Psalm 30:5 NASB

Be joyful always; pray continually; give thanks in all circumstances for this is God's will for you in Christ Jesus.
1 Thessalonians 5:16–18 NIV

Mirth is the sweet wine of human life. It should be offered sparkling with zestful life unto God.

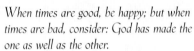

—HENRY WARD BEECHER

When times are good, be happy; but when times are bad, consider: God has made the one as well as the other.
Ecclesiastes 7:14 NIV

A joyful heart makes a cheerful face, But when the heart is sad, the spirit is broken.
Proverbs 15:13 NASB

Are any among you suffering? They should pray. Are any cheerful? They should sing songs of praise.
James 5:13 NRSV

A wife of noble character . . . can laugh at the days to come.
Proverbs 31:1, 25 NIV

Laughter is the most beautiful and beneficial therapy God ever granted humanity.

—CHARLES R. SWINDOLL

Snuggles

A Moment to Pause

Instead of automatically rolling to separate sides of the bed before drifting off to sleep, make a point tonight to scoot beyond the invisible line. Pile up the pillows on the bed and enjoy. Put your arms around each other and relax. Have a wind-down conversation and enjoy the sensation of drawing close to someone with whom you feel totally at ease.

The story is told that one four-year-old girl would, from time to time, approach her mom or dad and ask in her sweetest voice, "Would you snuggle me?" This little one was aware of her need to have someone draw her close.

Prepare yourself for a treat. Snuggling is a wonderfully intimate and comforting activity. Think of all the ways and all the places you have snuggled with your beloved: snuggling to music, snuggling to a movie or a TV program, snuggling close to your spouse while you read a good book, snuggling to poetry, snuggling to silence.

Snuggling and hugging can warm and refresh your soul. As the two of you snuggle together, see yourselves snuggling securely in God's arms. Feel him drawing you in and assuring you of his love. How blessed you are to be able to fall asleep secure in your spouse's arms.

Affection is responsible for nine-tenths of whatever solid and durable happiness there is in our lives.
—C. S. LEWIS

A Moment to Reflect

God does not physically snuggle with you, but he understands your need to experience love on the level of the senses, and he has given the two of you a common need for physical affection. He hugs each of you through the other.

When you snuggle up close to one another, you can experience the rest, security, and comfort that come from being loved unconditionally by each other and by God—fully accepted regardless of your faults and shortcomings. Physical affection is God's gift. Thank him for it, and thank him for the person he's chosen to snuggle you through.

Talk not of wasted affection!
Affection never was wasted;
If it enrich not the heart of another,
Its waters returning back to their springs,
Like the rain,
Shall fill them full of refreshment.

—Henry Wadsworth Longfellow

*You have been my refuge, a strong tower
against the foe.*

Psalm 61:3 NIV

A Moment to Refresh

Keep me safe, O God, for in you I take refuge.

Psalm 16:1 NIV

*"I will bring him near and he will come close to
me, for who is he who will devote himself to
me?" says the LORD.*

Jeremiah 30:21 NIV

*If you have any encouragement from being
united with Christ, if any comfort from his love,
if any fellowship with the Spirit, if any
tenderness and compassion, then make my joy
complete by being like-minded, having the same
love, being one in spirit and purpose.*

Philippians 2:1–2 NIV

*Surely it is you who love the people; all the holy
ones are in your hand. At your feet they all bow
down, and from you receive instruction.*

Deuteronomy 33:3 NIV

Thus hand in hand through life we'll go; its checker'd paths of joy and woe.

❧

—NATHANIEL COTTON

Place me like a seal over your heart, like a seal on your arm.

Song of Songs 8:6 NIV

May the Lord make your love increase and overflow for each other.

1 Thessalonians 3:12 NIV

He will cover you with his pinions, and under his wings you will find refuge.

Psalm 91:4 NRSV

I will sing to the LORD, for he has been good to me.

Psalm 13:6 NIV

Solomon said, "O LORD , God of Israel, there is no God like you in heaven above or on earth below—you who keep your covenant of love with your servants who continue wholeheartedly in your way."

1 Kings 8:23 NIV

The pain associated with emotional trials and worries can almost always be lessened by a little love.

❧

—CHRIS EDMUNDS

31

Blessed Verses

A Moment to Pause   Set aside some time today to read the Bible together. You might want to try doing this at the kitchen table with your morning cup of tea or coffee. Begin reading together by sharing your favorite scripture passages with each other. Identify what you feel is the primary verse in each passage and share what you find intriguing about it. Does it demonstrate God's power? Does it overflow with his love? Does it move you with compassion? Do you understand it in a new way?

Reading together like this can be an extraordinary experience. The Bible is a literary marvel and a poetic masterpiece. Its intrinsic value is incalculable. But even more amazing, the Bible is a letter written to you by your Creator, a letter expressing his love and commitment. From Genesis to Revelation, the Bible provides a detailed history of God's involvement with mankind. It also teaches principles for successful living and wisdom for dealing with others.

Expect to gain new awareness on a familiar aspect of your life or to find a solution for a problem you've been working through in your mind. The same passage can release different perspectives for each of you—perspectives that expand and deepen as you share them with each other.

The unfolding of your words gives light; it imparts understanding to the simple.
—PSALM 119:130 NRSV

A Moment to Reflect

The Bible is a particularly wonderful gift, in that it allows you to gain a glimpse of God— how he thinks, how he feels, how he wishes to be involved in your lives. The more you read his amazing letter, the more the two of you will know and understand about him and the more you will be drawn closer.

As you look into God's Word together, pray for understanding through God's Spirit. Take to heart the depth of his love for you expressed in its pages. It is the water of life for your souls.

The Bible is the light of my understanding, the joy of my heart, the fullness of my hope, the clarified of my affections, the mirror of my thoughts, the consoler of my sorrows, the guide of my soul through this gloomy labyrinth of time, the telescope went from heaven to reveal to the eye of man the amazing glories of the far distant world.

—Sir William Jones

33

Jesus said, "Blessed rather are those who hear the word of God and obey it."

Luke 11:28 NIV

A Moment to Refresh

Fix these words of mine in your hearts and minds; tie them as symbols on your hands and bind them on your foreheads.

Deuteronomy 11:18 NIV

Heaven and earth will pass away, but my words will never pass away.

Matthew 24:35 NIV

The word of God is living and active. Sharper than any double-edged sword, it penetrates even to dividing soul and spirit, joints and marrow; it judges the thoughts and attitudes of the heart.

Hebrews 4:12 NIV

Assemble the people before me to hear my words so that they may learn to revere me as long as they live in the land and may teach them to their children.

Deuteronomy 4:10 NIV

He will find one English book and one only, where perfect plainness of speech is allied with perfect nobleness; and that book is the Bible.

—MATTHEW ARNOLD

I treasure your word in my heart, so that I may not sin against you.

Psalm 119:11 NRSV

Jesus said, "If you continue in my word, you are truly my disciples; and you will know the truth, and the truth will make you free."

John 8:31–32 NRSV

All men are like grass, and all their glory is like the flowers of the field; the grass withers and the flowers fall, but the word of the Lord stands forever.

1 Peter 1:24–25 NIV

The word of the LORD came to Abram in a vision: "Do not be afraid, Abram. I am your shield, your very great reward."

Genesis 15:1 NIV

What power would come upon the soul if we would grasp a single line of Scripture and suck the honey out of it till our soul is filled with sweetness.

—C. H. SPURGEON

Three Little Words

A Moment to Pause Take a few minutes today to sit quietly with your spouse. Perhaps this time could be before you leave in the morning or when you get home in the evening or before you go to sleep at night. Look into each other's eyes and whisper these three powerful words, *I love you.*

I love you. Could anything your spouse says to you be any sweeter to hear, more comforting to know, more inspiring to lift you up? Think about it, and choose to keep those words a natural and everyday part of your interactions with each other. Choose to speak these tender words as often as you can. Make a personal commitment to say *I love you* as often as your heart recognizes the truth of those words.

As you express your love for each other, plan a special getaway just for the two of you—time alone to say those words and express your feelings for each other. Plan a leisurely walk in the park, a quiet dinner for two, an overnight stay at a hotel across town, or a special trip. Look forward to being together. Renew your commitment of love and fidelity by saying "I love you" often.

It is by loving and being loved that one can come nearest to the soul of another.
—GEORGE MACDONALD

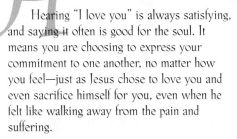

A Moment to Reflect

Hearing "I love you" is always satisfying, and saying it often is good for the soul. It means you are choosing to express your commitment to one another, no matter how you feel—just as Jesus chose to love you and even sacrifice himself for you, even when he felt like walking away from the pain and suffering.

Choose to continue to love each other more and more deeply as the years go by, and choose to express that commitment by saying those needed words as often as possible. Trust God to take your words and use them to strengthen and protect your relationship.

If ever two were one, then surely we.
If ever man were lov'd by wife, then thee;
If ever wife was happy in a man,
Compare with me ye women if you can.
Thy love is such I can no way repay,
The heavens reward thee manifold I pray.

—ANNE BRADSTREET

May the Lord direct your hearts into God's
love and Christ's perseverance.

2 Thessalonians 3:5 NIV

A Moment to Refresh

Many waters cannot quench love, neither can
floods drown it. If one offered for love all the
wealth of his house, it would be utterly scorned.

Song of Solomon 8:7 NRSV

Jesus said, "A new command I give you: Love
one another. As I have loved you, so you must
love one another."

John 13:34 NIV

The LORD appeared to us in the past, saying,
"I have loved you with an everlasting love; I
have drawn you with loving-kindness."

Jeremiah 31:3 NIV

I will sing of your strength, in the morning I
will sing of your love.

Psalm 59:16 NIV

Let love and faithfulness never leave you.

Proverbs 3:3 NIV

Such ever was love's way; to rise, it stoops.

—ROBERT BROWNING

Each one of you must love his wife as he loves himself, and the wife must respect her husband.

Ephesians 5:33 NIV

These three remain: faith, hope and love. But the greatest of these is love.

1 Corinthians 13:13 NIV

See what love the Father has given us, that we should be called children of God.

1 John 3:1 NRSV

Love and faithfulness meet together; righteousness and peace kiss each other.

Psalm 85:10 NIV

When I said, "My foot is slipping," your love, O LORD, supported me.

Psalm 94:18 NIV

Love all alike, no season knows, nor clime, nor hours, days, months, which are the rags of time.

—JOHN DONNE

Golden Circle

A Moment to Pause

Plan a double date with another couple, perhaps a couple from your church that you and your spouse like and feel comfortable with. Choose from a variety of options for this date—try out a new restaurant, attend a sporting event, see a new play at your community theater, go bowling, enjoy a picnic at a roadside park, take a walk on a wooded path, or sit in the backyard together for dessert and coffee.

Plan to use the time to give and receive insights, encouragement, and emotional support. Make conversation a central spot in your time together. Share your views and your values and discover your commonalities. Friendship is one of the richest and most satisfying relationships in life. Friends encourage the heart, stimulate the mind, and enhance the spirit. And when you two become friends with a like–minded couple, your time together can truly be a soul–enriching experience.

Spending time with friends will enrich your experience and spiritual growth as a couple and will add a new dimension to your relationship with your spouse. Your circle of two will be enhanced as you develop mutual friends and fuse yet one more important bond in your life together.

Life has no pleasure higher or nobler than that of friendship.

—SAMUEL JOHNSON

A Moment to Reflect

Jesus thought a lot of his friends. He spent time with them and shared his secrets with them. Jesus, the perfect man, appreciated the need for close friendships, and he set an important example as he chose his disciples and mingled with the people in his community.

Ask God to help you and your spouse find another couple with whom you can develop a strong friendship. Follow Jesus' example with your friends—he prayed for them, nurtured them, and made himself available to them. Praying for and supporting your friends and making yourself aware of their needs will gratify and unify you as a couple.

No medicine is more valuable, none more efficacious, none better suited to the cure of all our temporal ills than friends to whom we may turn for consolation in time of trouble—and with whom we may share our happiness in time of joy.

—Saint Aelred of Rievaulx

Iron sharpens iron, and one person sharpens the wits of another.

Proverbs 27:17 NRSV

A Moment to Refresh

I thank my God every time I remember you.

Philippians 1:3 NIV

If we walk in the light, as he is in the light, we have fellowship with one another.

1 John 1:7 NIV

A friend loves at all times.

Proverbs 17:17 NIV

Dear friends, since God so loved us, we also ought to love one another. No one has ever seen God; but if we love one another, God lives in us and his love is made complete in us.

1 John 4:11–12 NIV

I count myself in nothing else so happy as in a soul remembering my good friends.

ॐ

—William Shakespeare

Do not forsake your friend and the friend of your father, and do not go to your brother's house when disaster strikes you—better a neighbor nearby than a brother far away.

Proverbs 27:10 NIV

Jesus said, "I no longer call you servants, because a servant does not know his master's business. Instead, I have called you friends, for everything that I learned from my Father I have made known to you."

John 15:15 NIV

Abraham believed God, and it was credited to him as righteousness, and he was called God's friend.

James 2:23 NIV

A faithful friend is the medicine of life.

ॐ

—Apocrypha

A Double Hammock

A Moment to Pause Set aside some time today for the two of you to simply do nothing together. Find a couple of big, shady trees, tie up your hammock, and climb in together. Head for the beach and spread out your beach towels side by side in the sand. Snuggle up to each other on the sofa and watch some TV. Or take a nap together. Whatever you do, get off your feet and find refreshment.

Get the most from your rest time and tune out distractions of any stressful situations in your family or work life. Conversation won't be necessary as the two of you lie quietly together, each freeing herself and himself of obligations for this short respite. Rest invigorates the body, sharpens the mind, and soothes the soul.

Ah, sweet rest. You need it as certainly as you need food and water and vitamins and minerals. You may long for rest, at the same time you are aware that you often want and need more than what you get. Today you will enjoy the sweetness of that welcome relaxation—with the special bonus of sharing this time with the one you love. Rest is a God-thing, and you'll want to get your share.

One cannot rest except after steady practice.
GEORGE ADE

A Moment to Reflect

The Bible says that God created the world in six days and then set aside the seventh day for rest. God didn't need to rest, of course. But God's ingenious design for human beings calls for you to be renewed physically, mentally, and spiritually through rest. He set the example and established at the very beginning the habit of resting after labor.

God not only gives you license to rest, but he has also built the concept of rest into the process of work. As a couple, you will have many opportunities to work together. Follow these up with opportunities to rest together.

When, spurred by tasks unceasing or undone,
You would seek rest afar,
And cannot, though repose be rightly won—
Rest where you are.
Neglect the needless; sanctify the rest;
Move without stress or jar;
With quiet of spirit self-possessed—
Rest where you are.

—AUTHOR UNKNOWN

Six days you shall work, but on the seventh day you shall rest; even in plowing time and in harvest time you shall rest.

Exodus 34:21 NRSV

A Moment to Refresh

He makes me lie down in green pastures; he leads me beside still waters; he restores my soul.

Psalm 23:2–3 NRSV

They went away in a boat to a deserted place by themselves.

Mark 6:32 NRSV

Jesus said, "Come to me, all you who are weary and burdened, and I will give you rest."

Matthew 11:28 NIV

The LORD said, "My presence will go with you, and I will give you rest."

Exodus 33:14 NIV

Extreme busyness, whether at school or college, kirk or market,
is a symptom of deficient vitality.

—Robert Louis Stevenson

Because so many people were coming and going that they did not even have a chance to eat, [Jesus] said to them, "Come with me by yourselves to a quiet place and get some rest."

Mark 6:31 NIV

There remains, then, a Sabbath-rest for the people of God; for anyone who enters God's rest also rests from his own work, just as God did from his.

Hebrews 4:9–10 NIV

Jesus often withdrew to lonely places and prayed.

Luke 5:16 NIV

I shall have some peace there, for peace comes dropping slow, dropping from the veils of the morning to where the cricket sings.

—W. B. Yeats

What's for Dinner?

A Moment to Pause

Try something different today—form a culinary partnership. Pull out some cookbooks, and study them together. Consider an ethnic dish or something you'd only consider ordering in a restaurant. Or perhaps choose a longtime favorite that may require more time and hands than you usually have at your disposal.

Select a cookbook and choose a recipe. Now list the ingredients. Do you have everything you need? Make a quick trip to the grocery if needed, and then assemble the ingredients in little bowls on your work area. Go over the recipe together, deciding who will do what—who will chop, who will sauté, who will season, who will prepare the side vegetables.

Preparing a good, fresh meal is an art, one that can be creative and satisfying. Plan to serve your dinner on your best dishes with some well-placed candlelight and enjoy the satisfying experience.

God created you with senses that make the preparation of food and the process of eating a pleasurable experience, one that soothes, satisfies, and enriches the body and the soul. The aroma of a wonderful dish cooking in the oven, the rich colors on the plate, the taste and texture of the food as you eat it—all these produce a sense of well-being.

The discovery of a new dish does more for human happiness than the discovery of a star.
—ANTHELME BRILLAT-SAVARIN

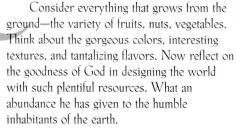

A Moment to Reflect

Consider everything that grows from the ground—the variety of fruits, nuts, vegetables. Think about the gorgeous colors, interesting textures, and tantalizing flavors. Now reflect on the goodness of God in designing the world with such plentiful resources. What an abundance he has given to the humble inhabitants of the earth.

As you rest from your labors and sit at the table, feast your senses on the bounty before you, take hands, pause for a moment, and thank God for his provision and for the joy of your partnership. Thank him for his care in giving the two of you such great pleasures in the most basic aspects of life.

No noisy crowds,
Beepers, or menus,
We're here together
In our very own venue,
Cooking exactly the fare we desire,
Eating in quiet, here by the fire.
Let's leave the dishes—
We'll clean up tomorrow.

—MOIRA ALLABY

*This is the way he governs the nations and
provides food in abundance.*

Job 36:31 NIV

A Moment to Refresh

*Nehemiah said, "Go and enjoy choice food and
sweet drinks, and send some to those who have
nothing prepared. This day is sacred to our
LORD.*

Nehemiah 8:10 NIV

*God said, "I give you every seed-bearing plant
on the face of the whole earth and every tree
that has fruit with seed in it. They will be yours
for food."*

Genesis 1:29 NIV

*You cause the grass to grow for the cattle, and
plants for people to use, to bring forth food from
the earth, and wine to gladden the human heart,
oil to make the face shine, and bread to
strengthen the human heart.*

Psalm 104:14–15 NRSV

Tell me what you eat: I will tell you what you are.

—JEAN-ANTHELME

*Everything God created is good, and
nothing is to be rejected if it is received with
thanksgiving.*

1 Timothy 4:4 NIV

*Whether you eat or drink or whatever you
do, do it all for the glory of God.*

1 Corinthians 10:31 NIV

*Jesus took some bread and gave thanks to
God in front of them all. Then he broke it
and began to eat.*

Acts 27:35 NIV

*Everything that lives and moves will be food
for you. Just as I gave you the green plants,
I now give you everything.*

Genesis 9:3 NIV

*That all-softening,
overpowering knell,
the tocsin of the
soul—the dinner
bell.*

—LORD BYRON

The Art of Noticing

A Moment to Pause Take a trip to the local card shop together to pick out perfect cards for each other. Giving and receiving expressions of appreciation and gratitude encourages the soul, and a carefully selected greeting card is a great way to do that.

Walk separately through the aisle, taking your time to find the appropriate card. Select one with a photo, design, or sentiment that communicates just how special your spouse is. When you get home, sit down across the table from each other and write what you are specifically grateful for inside the card. Perhaps it is his humor? Her gentleness? His stability? Her creativity? His working hard without complaint? Her keeping the household running seamlessly? When you're through, read the cards aloud to each other. Then exchange cards and read the other's card aloud.

Gratitude expressed toward your spouse says "I've noticed you. I've noticed the things that you do for me, the things you bring to my life. I've heard your words. I've seen your heart. I thank God for creating the completely unique and wonderful person you are." Few things will have an impact on your relationship so much as the deliberate expression of your gratitude for the person who shares your life and your love.

Gratitude is the memory of the heart.
—BILL VAUGHAN

A Moment to Reflect

Just as your spouse delights in gratitude for who he or she is, so does God delight in a heart grateful for him. Gratitude for all he is and does is one of the most significant aspects of praising God. When you make it a practice to continually express thanks to God, that attitude of gratefulness will pervade the other areas of your life.

When you lie down to sleep and when you wake with morning's light, thank God for the life he has given you. Allow thanks to underlie your words to God when you pray together. Acknowledge that you notice what God has promised, what he has given, and what he has done for you.

Haply I think on thee—and then my state,
Like to the lark at break of day arising
From sullen earth, sings hymns at heaven's gate;
For the sweet love remembered such
wealth brings
That then I scorn to change my state with kings.

— WILLIAM SHAKESPEARE

*Give thanks in all circumstances, for this is
God's will for you in Christ Jesus.*

1 Thessalonians 5:18 NIV

A Moment to Refresh

*The LORD God said, "It is not good that the
man should be alone; I will make him a helper
as his partner."*

Genesis 2:18 NRSV

*Each one of you also must love his wife as he
loves himself, and the wife must respect her
husband.*

Ephesians 5:33 NIV

*Let the peace of Christ rule in your hearts,
since as members of one body you were called
to peace. And be thankful.*

Colossians 3:15 NIV

*With praise and thanksgiving they sang to the
LORD: "He is good; his love to Israel endures
forever." And all the people gave a great shout
of praise to the LORD.*

Ezra 3:11 NIV

Gratitude looks to the past and love to the present.

—C. S. LEWIS

Let them sacrifice the sacrifices of thanksgiving, and declare his works with rejoicing.

Psalms 107:22 KJV

When you have eaten and are satisfied, praise the LORD your God.

Deuteronomy 8:10 NIV

Give thanks to the LORD, for he is good; his love endures forever.

1 Chronicles 16:34 NIV

Be thankful. Let the word of Christ dwell in you richly as you teach and admonish one another with all wisdom, and as you sing psalms, hymns and spiritual songs with gratitude in your hearts to God.

Colossians 3:15–16 NIV

The world is so full of a number of things, I'm sure we should all be as happy as kings.

—ROBERT LEWIS STEVENSON

Coffee and Conversation

A Moment to Pause Take a morning away, just the two of you and find a quiet spot. Whether under a shade tree, on a park bench, or in a quiet nook at a local café, settle in and get comfortable. Focus totally on your beloved. Speak to each other simply and freely, and speak only for the other's benefit. No one else is invited to this tête à tête. When the other is speaking, give your attention totally to what your partner is saying. Listening alertly and conscientiously is an art that might take a bit of practice, but the benefits are immeasurable.

Take turns encouraging each other to share thoughts on the important matters that transcend daily life. Talk about your faith in God and its importance in your life; talk about your hopes, your dreams, your future. Look into each other's eyes and ask gentle yet probing questions to make sure you understand what the other is saying. Pay total attention to your partner's words, making sure you don't start thinking about your response before he or she finishes speaking.

Many times—in the car, for instance, or while you're doing other things together—your attention may be divided. Make use of this special time to devote your attentions specifically and solely to your spouse.

The greatest gift you can give another is the
purity of your attention.
—RICHARD MOSS

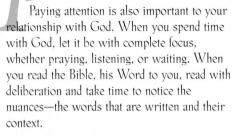

A Moment to Reflect Paying attention is also important to your relationship with God. When you spend time with God, let it be with complete focus, whether praying, listening, or waiting. When you read the Bible, his Word to you, read with deliberation and take time to notice the nuances—the words that are written and their context.

When you speak to God, you can be certain that his full attention is on you. He is never half-way listening, half-way seeing. He hears every word you speak and sees every intention of your heart. As you completely focus on him, he is completely focused on you.

God is a great listener.
Out of his silent being he is with us silently,
he speaks to us silently,
he asks us to learn the response
which comes from the deep part of our being.
He asks us to learn from him how to listen.

—MICHAEL HOLLINGS

The tongue of the wise brings healing.
Proverbs 12:18 NIV

A Moment to Refresh

Let everyone be quick to listen, slow to speak.
James 1:19 NRSV

Listen, for I have worthy things to say.
Proverbs 8:6 NIV

*Let your conversation be always full of grace,
seasoned with salt, so that you may know how
to answer everyone.*
Colossians 4:6 NIV

*Whoever gives heed to instruction prospers,
and blessed is he who trusts in the LORD. The
wise in heart are called discerning, and pleasant
words promote instruction.*
Proverbs 16:20–21 NIV

I neglect God and his Angels, for the noise of a fly, for the rattling of a coach, for the whining of a door.

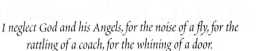

—JOHN DONNE

Pleasant words are as an honeycomb, sweet to the soul, and health to the bones.
                    Proverbs 16:24 KJV

A word fitly spoken is like apples of gold in pictures of silver.
                    Proverbs 25:11 KJV

This is the boldness we have in him, that if we ask anything according to his will, he hears us.
                    1 John 5:14 NRSV

Pay attention and listen to the sayings of the wise; apply your heart to what I teach, for it is pleasing when you keep them in your heart and have all of them ready on your lips.
                    Proverbs 22:17–18 NIV

She looked at him as one who awakes: The past was a sleep, and her life began.

—ROBERT BROWNING

Sharing a Book

A Moment to Pause

Sharing a book is great fun and an excellent way to learn about as well as from each other. To prepare for your soul retreat, venture out to your local bookstore or look online for a book that appeals to both of you. Open your hearts and minds to the possibility of a never-before-explored subject that you might not pursue on your own.

Think of it as an exclusive book club for two. You can simply exchange opinions or set up a specific forum, depending on the subject of the book. Check online resources through major distributors—many have discussion guides tailored to specific books. Tackle different types of reading, from a captivating mystery to a relevant religious or political commentary.

Depending on your style as a couple, you can enjoy the book at the same time—one person reading aloud and both sharing your thoughts as you go through the book. Or you may decide to read the book separately and then come together when you're finished to discuss the book.

Good books have the power to change, transform, and enlighten. When you share a book, its impact can be magnified, allowing each of you to incorporate the other's insights into your own experience.

When books are opened you discover
that you have wings.
—HELEN HAYES

A Moment to Reflect

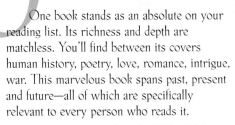

One book stands as an absolute on your reading list. Its richness and depth are matchless. You'll find between its covers human history, poetry, love, romance, intrigue, war. This marvelous book spans past, present and future—all of which are specifically relevant to every person who reads it.

This glorious book is the Bible. Well beyond its literary greatness, its words are God-breathed and have the power to instruct, transform, inspire, comfort, guide, and bring meaning and hope to your life together. As you make up your book list, include the Bible. Read it, study it, and take it to heart.

And nature, the old nurse, took
The child upon her knee,
Saying,"Here is a story book
My father hath writ for thee.
Come wander with me," she said,
"in regions yet untrod
and read what is still unread
in the manuscripts of God."

—HENRY WADSWORTH LONGFELLOW

The discerning heart seeks knowledge.
Proverbs 15:14 NIV

A Moment to Refresh

Everything that was written in the past was written to teach us, so that through endurance and the encouragement of the Scriptures we might have hope.
Romans 15:4 NIV

Happy is the one who reads this book, and happy are those who listen to the words of this prophetic message and obey that is written in this book!
Revelation 1:3 GNT

Pleasant words are like a honeycomb, sweet to the soul and healing to the bones.
Proverbs 16:24 NIV

You yourselves are full of goodness, complete in knowledge and competent to instruct one another. I have written you quite boldly on some points, as if to remind you of them again, because of the grace God gave me.
Romans 15:14–15 NIV

Books will speak plain when counsellors blanch.

—Francis Bacon

Let me understand the teaching of your precepts; then I will meditate on your wonders.

Psalm 119:27 NIV

The wise in heart are called discerning, and pleasant words promote instruction.

Proverbs 16:21 NIV

He gives wisdom to the wise and knowledge to the discerning. He reveals deep and hidden things; he knows what lies in darkness, and light dwells with him.

Daniel 2:21–22 NIV

Observe what the LORD your God requires: Walk in his ways, and keep his decrees and commands, his laws and requirements, as written in the Law of Moses, so that you may prosper in all you do and wherever you go.

1 Kings 2:3 NIV

No book is really worth reading at the age of ten, which is not equally (and often far more) worth reading at the age of fifty and beyond.

—C. S. Lewis

God's Provisions

A Moment to Pause Sometimes the best soul retreat is staying home, getting back in touch with your lives and with what you have together. Entertainment can be found at home as easily as it can be found away from home. But staying home comes with a bonus—great peace can be experienced by staying put and focusing on all the blessings God has given to you.

Set aside time to consciously focus in on what you have around you. Think about the simple things that you may take for granted and that may escape your notice in the busyness of everyday life—things like a warm bed, a healthy repast, a secure and pleasant place to live, the joy of waking refreshed, the blessing of good health, and loving family you have around you.

Relish that early morning cup of coffee and the freedom you have to make choices so simple and valued as what you'll have to eat. Take time to enjoy your blessings. Talk together about what God has provided for you. As the old hymn states, "count your blessings," naming them specifically. As you do, thank God for all he has done, for all of the ways in which he has provided for you, from your possessions to the people in your life, and especially for each other.

Each day comes bearing its own gifts.
Untie the ribbons.
—RUTH ANN SCHABACKER

A Moment to Reflect

While you are counting your physical and material blessings, remember to thank God for the ways he has blessed you spiritually. Thank him for his nurturance and his provision for your inner selves as well as your outer selves. While your physical and material blessings are only for this life, your spiritual blessings are eternal. They will always be there.

There is no greater blessing than the forgiveness of sins and the gift of eternal life provided for you through Jesus, God's Son. God's presence is always with you, watching over you, comforting you, guiding you, instructing you, and loving you.

This newborn day
Offering up an unblemished canvas,
An unwritten book
So singularly unique, it seems it was
Made just for us,
God's simple blessing.

ॐ

—*Tara Afriat*

Remember the LORD your God, for it is he who gives you power to get wealth.

Deuteronomy 8:18 NRSV

A Moment to Refresh

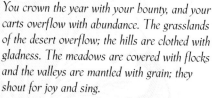

You crown the year with your bounty, and your carts overflow with abundance. The grasslands of the desert overflow; the hills are clothed with gladness. The meadows are covered with flocks and the valleys are mantled with grain; they shout for joy and sing.

Psalm 65:11–13 NIV

We have both straw and provender enough, and room to lodge in. And the man bowed down his head, and worshipped the LORD.

Genesis 24:25–26 KJV

You would be fed with the finest of wheat; with honey from the rock I would satisfy you.

Psalm 81:16 NIV

All that we have of soul and body, whatever we possess interiorly or exteriorly, by nature or by grace, are Your gifts and they proclaim Your goodness and mercy from which we have received all good things.

—THOMAS À KEMPIS

Give thanks unto the LORD, call upon his name, make known his deeds among the people. Sing unto him, sing psalms unto him, talk ye of all his wondrous works.
1 Chronicles 16:8–9 KJV

The LORD is good; His lovingkindness is ever-lasting, And his faithfulness to all generations.

Psalm 100:5 NASB

Thanks be to God for his indescribable gift!
2 Corinthians 9:15 NIV

You will eat the fruit of your labor; blessings and prosperity will be yours.
Psalm 128:2 NIV

Those blessings are sweetest that are won with prayers and worn with thanks.

—THOMAS GOODWIN

Sometimes Solo

A Moment to Pause Talk it over with your spouse and together choose a day to be spent apart from each other. And then each of you make it entirely your own. Depending on the dynamics of your life (such as children or other caretaking responsibilities), you may have to take separate days. Do the thing that perhaps you enjoy, and your partner doesn't, hanging out in the bookstore for an afternoon or on the golf course. Whatever it is, make sure it's relaxing and in some way helping you to refuel. Be sure to take some time during the day to be alone with your thoughts, encouraging your unique personal creativity.

Couples need time together, varied between fun, business, serious conversation, relaxation, and other activities, in order for their relationship to flourish. But sometimes, togetherness is heavenly and time alone, divine. Dynamic relationships also need time for partners to nurture their own individuality.

Much of how you approach a day, an hour, or a situation depends on your perspective and your own sense of inner peace and confidence. It is only by drawing away that you gain clear vision. Time by yourself is an unselfish gift you can give each other that will bless your relationship a hundredfold.

Jesus knows we must come apart and rest
awhile, or else we may just come apart.
— VANCE HAVNER

A Moment to Reflect

Spending time praying and reading God's Word as a couple is powerful. It is also important that each of you spend time with God alone in prayer and Bible-reading. God wants to have a vibrant personal relationship with each of you.

The marvel of it all is that the time you spend with God alone serves to strengthen and enhance your relationship with each other. Each of you will gain new insights and understanding about God and rejoice in sharing them with the other. Find time to get alone with God and give him your full focus.

I long for scenes where man has never trod;
A place where woman never smiled or wept;
There to abide with my Creator, God,
And sleep as I in childhood sweetly slept;
Untroubling and untroubled where I lie;
The grass below—above the vaulted sky.

—JOHN CLARE

Jesus said, "Come to me, all you who are
weary and burdened, and I will give you rest."
Matthew 11:28 NIV

A Moment to Refresh

When Jesus heard what had happened, he
withdrew by boat privately to a solitary place.
Matthew 14:13 NIV

For God alone my soul waits in silence; from
him comes my salvation.
Psalm 62:1 NRSV

Let us examine our ways and test them, and let
us return to the LORD.
Lamentations 3:40 NIV

God, who searches the heart, knows what is the
mind of the Spirit, because the Spirit intercedes
for the saints according to the will of God.
Romans 8:27 NRSV

Anyone, then, who aims to live the inner and spiritual life must go apart, with Jesus, from the crowd.

—THOMAS À KEMPIS

Draw nigh to God, and he will draw nigh to you.

James 4:8 KJV

Jesus often withdrew to lonely places and prayed.

Luke 5:16 NIV

The LORD said, "Be still, and know that I am God: I will be exalted among the heathen, I will be exalted in the earth."

Psalm 46:10 KJV

I will lie down and sleep in peace, for you alone, O LORD, make me dwell in safety.

Psalm 4:8 NIV

True religion disposes persons to be much alone in solitary places for holy meditation and prayer.

—JONATHAN EDWARDS

Expressing Your Heart

A Moment to Pause   Find pen and paper, and then each of you move away to your own quiet spot. For this retreat, you will be writing love letters to each other. Expressing your love on paper is a wonderful way to connect with each other, to delight and inspire each other, to convey your love for each other.

Before you begin, think about your relationship—what drew you together, captured your heart, made you notice each other? How has your love grown? What have you discovered about the person you love that has given you more respect for him or her? Set pen to paper and begin to write. Write as many drafts as you want—the writers of most of the famous love poems rewrote until they were pleased. When you are satisfied that you have said what you wanted, exchange letters. Read and reflect on your beloved's words.

Writing a love letter is almost a lost art, and yet it is so pleasurable for both writer and recipient. Expressing your tender feelings of love for someone requires vulnerability—once your words are on paper, they are down there for your beloved to keep, perhaps for years. Make your words something he or she will cherish.

Love letters are the campaign promises
of the heart.
—Robert Friedman

A Moment to Reflect

Romantic love is an incredible and powerful gift from God. The magnetic pull that draws two people to each other and leads them to want to spend their lives together is an amazing mystery, hard to fathom but joyous to discover.

As you think about and write to your spouse, thank God for the privilege of sharing life with his unique and beautifully complex creation. Include that thankfulness in the body of your love letter. Let your spouse know that you are grateful to God for the person he or she is and for placing him or her in your life.

With these words, I present
To thee what I most owe.
My heart and all it doth contain
Love's tender flowers yet unsown.
With trembling hand, I pen
Each passionate thought
As silver under the smithy's care
Love's shimmering treasure now is wrought.

—ANDREA GARNEY

We love because he first loved us.

1 John 4:19 NIV

A Moment to Refresh

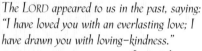

*The LORD appeared to us in the past, saying:
"I have loved you with an everlasting love; I
have drawn you with loving-kindness."*

Jeremiah 31:3 NIV

*Place me like a seal over your heart, like a seal
on your arm; for love is as strong as death . . .
Many waters cannot quench love; rivers cannot
wash it away. If one were to give all the wealth
of his house for love, it would be utterly
scorned.*

Song of Songs 8:6, 7 NIV

*Owe nothing to anyone except to love one
another.*

Romans 13:8 NASB

*Love one another warmly as Christians, and be
eager to show respect for one another.*

Romans 12:10 GNT

74

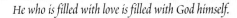

He who is filled with love is filled with God himself.

—*Saint Augustine of Hippo*

Above all, maintain constant love for one another.

1 Peter 4:8 NRSV

Be imitators of God, as beloved children, and live in love, as Christ loved us and gave himself up for us, a fragrant offering and sacrifice to God.

Ephesians 5:1–2 NRSV

There is nothing in all creation that will ever be able to separate us from the love of God which is ours through Christ Jesus our Lord.

Romans 8:39 GNT

Let all that you do be done in love.

1 Corinthians 16:14 NASB

Only love can bring individual beings to their perfect completion as individuals because only love takes possession of them and unites them by what lies deepest within them.

—*Pierre Teilhard de Chardin*

Expanding Your Horizons

A Moment to Pause   Set aside some time and talk together about what you've always wanted to do. Discuss facets of your life that you'd like to broaden. Pursuing a new endeavor together is a wonderful way to introduce something inspiring, energizing, and invigorating into your relationship.

Some possibilities might include learning to speak Spanish, to dance the foxtrot or the tango, to work with stained glass, or to figure out how to burn CDs on your new computer. Maybe it's a long-time personal dream that you had given up on or decided was too impractical. Or it could be something that you would like to learn to do together—such as a particular hobby or craft. Relax and have fun as you consider your choices.

Share what you'd like to do with your spouse, and talk about the reasons why that particular subject appeals to you. Then listen to what he or she would like to do. After you've both talked, settle on one idea from each person that you have agreed to jointly pursue.

Before your retreat time is finished, take the list in your hands and pray over it. Ask God to help you enjoy your new ventures as learn together.

What we learn with pleasure, we never forget.
—ALFRED MERCIER

A Moment to Reflect The Bible cites many instances when God did amazing things through people who were out of their "comfort zones." Some willingly stepped out, and others God simply placed outside of the familiar routines of their lives.

God can and will use you as you step out to learn new things in a sense of adventure. Pray about ways to use your newfound skills in ways that will please him and bless the lives of others. And be willing to reach out beyond the mastering of some new skill to the application of that skill for the betterment of yourselves and others.

Education is the leading of human souls to what is best, and making what is best out of them; and these two objects are always attainable together, and by the same means' the training which makes men happiest in themselves also makes them most serviceable to others.

—JOHN RUSKIN

Let us discern for ourselves what is right; let us learn together what is good.

Job 34:4 NIV

A Moment to Refresh

Apply your mind to instruction and your ear to words of knowledge.

Proverbs 23:12 NRSV

Give instruction to the wise, and they will become wiser still.

Proverbs 9:9 NRSV

The Lord is the Spirit, and where the Spirit of the Lord is, there is freedom.

2 Corinthians 3:17 NIV

Let the wise listen and add to their learning, and let the discerning get guidance—for understanding proverbs and parables, the sayings and riddles of the wise.

Proverbs 1:5–6 NIV

[Knowledge is] a rich storehouse for the glory of the Creator, and the relief of man's estate.

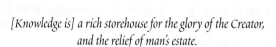

—Francis Bacon

Sing unto him a new song; play skillfully, and shout for joy.

Psalm 33:3 NIV

A wise man will hear, and will increase learning; and a man of understanding shall attain unto wise counsels.

Proverbs 1:5 KJV

Hold on to instruction, do not let it go; guard it well, for it is your life.

Proverbs 4:13 NIV

Instruct a wise man and he will be wiser still; teach a righteous man and he will add to his learning. The fear of the LORD is the beginning of wisdom, and knowledge of the Holy One is understanding.

Proverbs 9:9–10 NIV

The main part of intellectual education is not the acquisition of facts but learning how to make facts live.

—Oliver Wendell Holmes Jr.

Soaking It Up

A Moment to Pause Take some time together, get out in the sun, and do something you both enjoy. Take a walk through a meadow or hike up a mountainside. Pump up your bicycle tires and go for a spin or simply stretch out side by side on a couple of deck chairs. Turn your faces to the sky, soaking up the golden rays. Feel the sun envelop you; feel its heat moving over you.

You can also enjoy the sun in other ways—the blazing spectrum of color in the dusk sky, the dancing light bouncing off a mountain snowfall, the blazing ball edging over the horizon, the comforting warmth of sunshine on your face, your back, your shoulders. The sun enlivens your senses in a special way.

The sun, in moderation, is known to have a positive effect on the human body, stimulating circulation and causing the release of endorphins in the brain to ward off depression. Its very presence brings order to life simply by lending its predictable routines. The sun pales in comparison to its Creator, the Lord God. God placed the sun in the sky to warm the earth and make it a fitting place to live.

Is it so small a thing to have enjoyed the sun, to have lived light in the spring, to have loved, to have thought, to have done?

MATTHEW ARNOLD

A Moment to Reflect

In the Bible, Jesus is called the Sun of Righteousness. This comparison to the sun that sits in the center of our universe is no coincidence. For just as the sunshine warms the earth and gives it life, the love of God through Jesus his Son can warm your hearts and give you life. His presence in your lives drives away the darkness and provides order and meaning.

God has given you all you need to sustain physical life and spiritual life. Thank him for the sunshine and take every opportunity you can to soak up its rich benefits.

The heavens declare the glory of God; the skies proclaim the work of his hands ... In the heavens he has pitched a tent for the sun, which is like a bridegroom coming forth from his pavilion, like a champion rejoicing to run his course. It rises at one end of the heavens and makes its circuit to the other; nothing is hidden from its heat.

—*PSALM 19:1, 4–6 NIV*

From the rising of the sun to its setting the name of the LORD is to be praised.

Psalm 113:3 NRSV

A Moment to Refresh

The LORD Almighty says, "For you who obey me, my saving power will rise on you like the sun and bring healing like the sun's rays."

Malachi 4:2 GNT

When I consider your heavens, the work of your fingers, the moon and the stars, which you have set in place, what is man that you are mindful of him, the son of man that you care for him?

Psalm 8:3–4 NIV

He hath made every thing beautiful in his time: also he hath set the world in their heart, so that no man can find out the work that God maketh from the beginning to the end.

Ecclesiastes 3:11 KJV

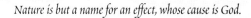

Nature is but a name for an effect, whose cause is God.

—WILLIAM COWPER

*God made two great lights—the greater
light to govern the day and the lesser light
to govern the night. He also made the stars.
God set them in the expanse of the sky to
give light on the earth, to govern the day
and the night, and to separate light from
darkness. And God saw that it was good.*

Genesis 1:16–18 NIV

*Praise God, sun and moon; praise him, all
you shining stars! Praise him, you highest
heavens, and you waters above the heavens!*

Psalm 148:3–4 NRSV

*The LORD God is a sun and shield: the
LORD will give grace and glory: no good
thing will he withhold from them that walk
uprightly.*

Psalm 84:11 KJV

*Goodness comes
out of people who
bask in the sun, as it
does out of a sweet
apple roasted before
the fire.*

—CHARLES DUDLEY
WARNER

Look What You've Done

A Moment to Pause Take some special time apart to relive your accomplishments together, such as the birth of your children, your graduation from a special course, the last payment on your mortgage, or the triumph over a disability. Bring to mind the satisfaction you felt. Mentally rehearse the part each of you played. Maybe she worked while you studied or he gave you the encouragement to start your own business.

Choose two or three accomplishments and think about them in detail, recalling your motivations, hard work, and perseverance. When you were young, if you were like most children, you would jump at the chance to show the adults in your life what you achieved. Perhaps you can recall running to Dad with a school paper that sported a bright sticker or shouting for Mom to look as you sprang off the diving board.

Recalling the accomplishments of the past will inspire you to pursue dreams yet unfulfilled. As adults, you may be more reticent to proclaim your accomplishments to the world or to each other. However, with all that life requires, especially the work that goes into a relationship between a man and woman, know that it's important to stop and take stock of your successes as a couple.

*Out of the strain of the Doing, into the
peace of the Done.*
—JULIA LOUISE WOODRUFF

A Moment to Reflect

As you reflect on your accomplishments, include spiritual milestones. Do you recall the moment when each of you turned your back on sin and became a child of God? Do you remember the time when a crisis tested your faith, and you trusted God to bring you through it? How about the time you persisted together in prayer, refusing to let go until the answer came? God remembers all these things.

And there's something else—accomplishments in your spiritual lives have staying power. They are eternal. Even after you have both left this world to take up residence in heaven, you will be able to celebrate your spiritual accomplishments together.

Four steps to achievement:

Plan purposefully.

Prepare prayerfully.

Proceed positively.

Pursue persistently.

ثC

—WILLIAM A. WARD

85

Whatever your hand finds to do, do it with all your might.

Ecclesiastes 9:10 NIV

A Moment to Refresh

Stand firm. Let nothing move you. Always give yourselves fully to the work of the Lord, because you know that your labor in the Lord is not in vain.

1 Corinthians 15:58 NIV

His lord said unto him, Well done, good and faithful servant; thou hast been faithful over a few things, I will make thee ruler over many things: enter thou into the joy of thy lord.

Matthew 25:23 KJV

Seeing we also are compassed about with so great a cloud of witnesses, let us lay aside every weight, and the sin which doth so easily beset us, and let us run with patience the race that is set before us.

Hebrews 12:1 KJV

Something attempted, something done, has earned a night's repose.

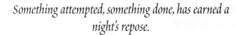

—HENRY WADSWORTH LONGFELLOW

Let us not become weary in doing good, for at the proper time we will reap a harvest if we do not give up.

Galatians 6:9 NIV

I have fought the good fight, I have finished the race, I have kept the faith.

2 Timothy 4:7 NIV

The LORD said, My word "will not return to me empty, but will accomplish what I desire and achieve the purpose for which I sent it. You will go out in joy and be led forth in peace; the mountains and hills will burst into song before you, and all the trees of the field will clap their hands."

Isaiah 55:11–12 NIV

It is not the going out of port, but the coming in, that determines the success of a voyage.

—HENRY WARD BEECHER

87

The Sweetness of Song

A Moment to Pause

Perhaps the two of you have a special memory relating to a song, "your" song, or you both enjoy a certain group or artist or a particular type of music, like pop or country or gospel. Whatever that music is, select the CD or tune in your favorite music station and make yourselves comfortable while you experience once again those wonderful emotions that hearing your music brings.

Sit close while you listen. Let the music wash over you, enfold you. Close your eyes and remember those milestones in your relationship that the music brings to mind. If your tunes are danceable, get up and move. If your music has words, sing to each other. Let your hearts recapture those moments of first love and commitment that brought you together. Keep listening and responding, holding on to the old memories while your hearts reach for new ones.

Music makes a strong and lasting impression, especially when it is part of a special moment or occasion between two people. Music expresses the heart and touches the mind and emotions. So retreat into each other's arms with the music you both love. Enjoy the bonding it brings to your relationship and the refreshment it provides for your souls.

Music is the way our memories sing to us
across time.
—LANCE MORROW

A Moment to Reflect

The Bible says that music was created for the purpose of praising and worshiping God, and that angels are assigned to sing and play instruments constantly around his throne. No wonder music has such amazing qualities, such as its ability to evoke emotion and inspire loving thoughts. Music is a natural part of every vital, living relationship with God.

As you use music to draw closer to each other, allow it also to draw you closer to God, who created you and your music in the first place. It will enhance your awareness and appreciation of God and your sense of his presence.

How sweet the moonlight sleeps upon this bank!
Here will we sit, and let the sounds of music
Creep in our ears: soft stillness and the night
Become the touches of sweet harmony.

—WILLIAM SHAKESPEARE

Sing and make music in your heart to the Lord.
Ephesians 5:19 NIV

A Moment to Refresh

You will have songs as in the night when you keep the festival, And gladness of heart as when one marches to the sound of the flute.
Isaiah 30:29 NASB

Awake harp and lyre! I will awaken the dawn. I will praise you, O LORD, among the nations.
Psalm 108:2–3 NIV

David and all the house of Israel were celebrating before the LORD with all kinds of instruments made of fir wood, and with lyres, harps, tambourines, castanets and cymbals.
2 Samuel 6:5 NASB

Hear this, you kings! Listen, you rulers! I will sing to the LORD, I will sing; I will make music to the LORD, the God of Israel.
Judges 5:3 NIV

O Music! Thou bringest the receding waves of eternity nearer to the weary soul.

—Johann Paul Friedrich Richter

Sing to the LORD a new song, his praise from the end of the earth!
Isaiah 42:10 NRSV

Sing to him a new song; play skillfully on the strings, with loud shouts.
Psalm 33:3 NRSV

Shout with joy to God, all the earth!
Psalm 66:1 NIV

Sing praises to God, sing praises; sing praises to our King, sing praises. For God is the King of all the earth; sing to him a psalm of praise.
Psalm 47:6–7 NIV

Music is God's best gift to man. The only art of heaven given to earth, the only art of earth we take to heaven.

—Letitia Elizabeth Landon

Renewed Vows

A Moment to Pause   The next time you're invited to a wedding ceremony, make it a special retreat for your souls that transcends the gift giving, dressing up, and going to a good party. As you hear the other couple recite their vows, promising to love and respect and cherish each other forever and ever, take the opportunity to renew and affirm your own love and commitment for each other.

Hold hands to create a special sense of connectedness. Listen to the minister's words and draw insights from them that you can incorporate into your own marriage. Silently reflect on the vows being spoken and claim them once more for your own marriage. Know that you will leave the celebration with a sense of strengthened commitment and renewed love for each other.

As you renew your commitment to each other, thank God. Thank him for helping you find your beloved, thank him for encouraging your love to grow, and thank him for having guided you through the days, weeks, months, or years since you first said your vows. Thank God for keeping your love and commitment strong as you continue to walk together through the remainder of your lives.

The resolved mind hath no cares.
—GEORGE HERBERT

A Moment to Reflect

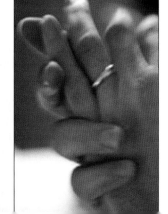

Your commitment to God is in many ways similar to the commitment that is made in earthly marriage. The correlation is so strong that those who commit their lives to Jesus Christ, God's Son, and vow to live in a spiritual covenant relationship with him are referred to in the Bible as his bride.

The vow you made to God should also be renewed often. Each time you enter a place of worship—a church, a garden, the spot where you kneel at the foot of your bed, take time to say, "Lord, I love you. I renew my commitment to you afresh and promise to continue in vital relationship with you today and in the all the days to come."

The most wonderful of all things in life, I believe, is the discovery of another human being with whom one's relationship has a glowing depth, beauty and joy as the years increase. This inner progressiveness of love between two human beings is a most marvelous thing, it cannot be found by looking for it or by passionately wishing for it. It is a sort of Divine accident.

—Sir Hugh Walpole

93

My foot has held fast to His path; I have kept
His way and not turned aside.

Job 23:11 NASB

A Moment to Refresh

Let endurance have its perfect result, that you
may be perfect and complete, lacking in nothing.

James 1:4 NASB

Give ear and come to me; hear me, that your
soul may live. I will make an everlasting
covenant with you.

Isaiah 55:3 NIV

When a man makes a vow to the LORD or
takes an oath to obligate himself by a pledge, he
must not break his word but must do everything
he said.

Numbers 30:2 NIV

The wife's body does not belong to her alone
but also to her husband. In the same way, the
husband's body does not belong to him alone
but also to his wife.

1 Corinthians 7:4 NIV

Successful marriage is always a triangle,
a man, a woman, and God.

ॐ

—CECIL MYERS

For this reason a man shall leave his father
and mother, and shall be joined to his wife;
and the two shall become one flesh. This
mystery is great.

Ephesians 5:31–32 NASB

Create a pure heart, O God, and renew a
steadfast spirit within me.

Psalm 51:10 NIV

Do not let loyalty and faithfulness forsake
you; bind them around your neck, write
them on the tablet of your heart.

Proverbs 3:3 NRSV

Each one of you also must love his wife as
he loves himself, and the wife must respect
her husband.

Ephesians 5:33 NIV

Pundits and
politicians offer a lot
of "shoulds" and
"oughts" about
marriage, but what
we don't hear
enough about is the
sheer joy and delight
of committed love.

ॐ

—PAT LOVE

Working It Out

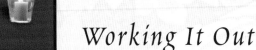

A Moment to Pause

Set aside some time today to explore and encourage your faith to grow by finding a practical definition you agree on and recalling how faith has worked in your lives in the past. Sit down across from each other and write out your individual definitions of faith—what you believe it to be. When you have finished, read your definitions out loud. Now consider this dictionary definition: belief that isn't based on proof. Discuss how your definitions compare to this one.

Open your Bible and read Hebrews 11:1: "Now faith is being sure of what we hope for and certain of what we do not see" (NIV). What do you think about this definition? How does it compare with the definitions you've written? In what way does the Bible definition differ from the dictionary definition?

Once you've decided how you define faith, discuss some of the instances when you feel faith was at work in your lives. Growing together in faith individually and as a couple is one of the greatest investments you can make in your future A living, active faith in God is a mighty tool. It makes the weak strong and the frightened brave. It changes hate to love and failure to victory.

It is the heart that experiences God,
and not the reason.

—*BLAISE PASCAL*

A Moment to Reflect

Human beings place their faith in all kinds of things—money, fame, education, social standing, to name a few. But faith is only sure when it is placed in God. Only God can absolutely guarantee what you entrust to him.

As you take time together to reflect on the role faith plays in your lives, keep your eyes firmly focused on him and anchored in his wisdom and love. Everything and everyone else will fail you, regardless of how hopeful and pure their intention might be. No matter how safe and secure the thing you're trusting in might seem.

Faith is the soul's eye by which it sees the Lord. Faith is the soul's ear by which we hear what God will speak. Faith is the spiritual hand, which touches and grasps the things not seen as yet. Faith is the spiritual nostril, which perceives the precious perfume of our Lord's garments.

—CHARLES H. SPURGEON

Faith is the assurance of things hoped for, the
conviction of things not seen.

Hebrews 11:1 NASB

A Moment to Refresh

It is by grace you have been saved, through
faith—and this not from yourselves, it is the gift
of God.

Ephesians 2:8 NIV

Jesus said, "Whatever you ask for in prayer,
believe that you have received it, and it will be
yours."

Mark 11:24 NRSV

Jesus said, "If you have faith as a mustard seed,
you shall say to this mountain, move from here
to there, and it shall move; and nothing shall be
impossible to you."

Matthew 17:20 NASB

Hope is putting faith to work when doubting would be easier.

—AUTHOR UNKNOWN

Since we have been justified through faith, we have peace with God through our Lord Jesus Christ.

Romans 5:1 NIV

In Christ Jesus neither circumcision nor uncircumcision has any value. The only thing that counts is faith expressing itself through love.

Galatians 5:6 NIV

In the gospel a righteousness from God is revealed, a righteousness that is by faith from first to last, just as it is written: "The righteous will live by faith."

Romans 1:17 NIV

Faith is an awareness of divine mutuality and companionship, a form of communion between God and man.

—ABRAHAM JOSHUA HESCHEL

Enough Distance to See

A Moment to Pause

Take a little time apart today for some personal discovery and reflection. Lounge in separate parts of the house or under separate trees in the yard. Walk down separate paths or get into your cars and head off in different directions. Make this a time when your perceptions are truly your own. In order to bring the very best of yourself to your relationship, you must have time to know yourself, your thoughts, your motivations, your opinions.

You can enhance your time alone by deciding on two or three issues on which you need insight. That might be having a family, changing careers, or choosing a church, perhaps. Take your Bible along with you to your alone place. Once you are settled and feeling relaxed, pray that God will make the picture clear for you. Read from one of the Gospels. Now tackle your concerns. Allow your thoughts to be free and unreserved. Entertain new ideas. Consider possible conclusions.

When your mental debate is finished, rest your mind and listen with your heart until you can see clearly. Then jot down your insights so that you can share them with your spouse later. Your time alone will bring additional strength and clarity to your lives together.

Climb up on some hill at sunrise. Everybody needs perspective once in a while, and you'll find it there.

ROBB SAGENDORPH

A Moment to Reflect

Getting away to focus can be a productive way to gain perspective. But God has given you another tool with which to gain and keep the proper outlook on life. That gift is the Bible—God's Word. As you read, you will find you have greater clarity concerning how you should live, how you can improve your relationships, and how to know which things in life are really important.

God's Word serves as a standard by which you can judge the purity and truth of your opinions both as an individual and as a couple. As you set out to put things in perspective, take time to draw from its constant and timeless wisdom.

If I had time to find a place
And sit down quietly and face
My better self, which cannot show
Because my days are crowded so;
And see my distant gleaming goal,
It might be I should find my soul.
And even thrill with thought sublime,
If I could only find the time.

—AUTHOR UNKNOWN

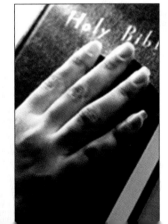

I will give you a new heart and put a new spirit in you.

Ezekiel 36:26 NIV

A Moment to Refresh

The law of the Lord is perfect, reviving the soul.

Psalm 19:7 NIV

Jesus said, "Neither do men pour new wine into old wineskins. If they do, the skins will burst, the wine will run out and the wineskins will be ruined. No, they pour new wine into new wineskins, and both are preserved."

Matthew 9:17 NIV

Restore to me the joy of your salvation, and sustain in me a willing spirit.

Psalm 51:12 NSRV

God gave Solomon wisdom and very great insight, and a breadth of understanding as measureless as the sand on the seashore.

1 Kings 4:29 NIV

God's perspective is always perfect. And those who ask with a pure heart are sometimes given a glimpse of the world through his eyes.

—ANDREA GARNEY

If anyone is in Christ, there is a new creation: everything old has passed away; see, everything has become new!
2 Corinthians 5:17 NRSV

He restores my soul. He guides me in paths of righteousness for his name's sake.
Psalm 23:3 NIV

Your attitude should be the same as that of Christ Jesus
Philippians 2:5 NIV

I have seen his ways, but I will heal him; I will guide him and restore comfort to him.
Isaiah 57:18 NIV

Your hands made me and formed me; give me understanding to learn your commands.
Psalm 119:73 NIV

Boldly say each night, To-morrow let my sun his beams display, or in clouds hide them; I have lived to-day.

—ABRAHAM COWLEY

Hand in Hand

A Moment to Pause   Take some time today to think about security. Most couples spend a lot of time planning it and a lot of money buying it, especially as the years go by—secure investments, secure income, security systems to protect what they have. Now consider whether security is a realistic goal. Take your spouse's hand and for a few moments talk about your answers to this question: How secure are the lives we now live? Think about the different types of insurance that you have: mortgage, health, car, disability, life. You probably have a fairly complete list of policies.

The simple truth is, it's impossible to be prepared for everything. Life is unpredictable. Discuss your answers to these questions: Whom can we look to when all our earthly security fails? Who is our last line of defense? Our family? Each other? Or God?

Now, as partners in life, pray together and agree together to base your security in almighty God. The psalmist said that God pulled his feet from the miry clay and set him upon a rock. He probably never thought he would need "clay" insurance, but when he got stuck, God was there to help him recover from foolish mistakes and find a safe haven from his enemies. He will be there for you too. You can depend on it.

Security is not the absence of danger, but the presence of God, no matter what the danger.

—AUTHOR UNKNOWN

A Moment to Reflect

You may feel like you have your bases covered and you are prepared for any extremity this life has to offer. But what about the life to come? What about eternity?

Only God can offer you eternal security. He purchased the insurance once and for all with the blood of his Son, Jesus Christ, which was spilled for you on the Cross. Be as wise to plan for eternity as you have been to plan for this life. Take the hand of the Savior and ask him to grant you eternal salvation. You can't be more secure than that.

God is over all things, under all things; outside all; within but not enclosed; without but not excluded; above but not raised up; below but not depressed, wholly above, presiding; wholly beneath, sustaining; wholly without, embracing; wholly within, filling.

—*Hildebert of Lavardin*

This God is our God for ever and ever; he will be our guide even to the end.

Psalm 48:14 NIV

A Moment to Refresh

Having been justified by his grace, we might become heirs having the hope of eternal life.

Titus 3:7 NIV

The name of the LORD is a strong tower; the righteous run into it and are safe.

Proverbs 18:10 NRSV

Let all who take refuge in you rejoice; let them ever sing for joy. Spread your protection over them, so that those who love your name may exult in you.

Psalm 5:11 NRSV

I will heal my people and will let them enjoy abundant peace and security.

Jeremiah 33:6 NIV

One of the outstanding glories of the gospel is its promise of eternal security to all who truly believe it.

❧

—A. W. PINK

We have this hope as an anchor for our soul, firm and secure.

Hebrews 6:19 NIV

He will have no fear of bad news; his heart is steadfast, trusting in the LORD.

Psalm 112:7 NIV

By grace you have been saved through faith, and this is not your own doing; it is the gift of God.

Ephesians 2:8 NRSV

May there be peace within your walls and security within your citadels.

Psalm 122:7 NIV

With God, we have nothing to fear—not even fear itself.

❧

—NAVA WHITE

Remembering Us

A Moment to Pause Earmark this retreat for a time when you are both feeling that life is routine and dull. When you feel that way, put down the paper, turn off the TV, and curl up on the couch together with your most precious keepsakes of your life together—picture albums, letters, and souvenirs.

Spread out these mementos before you, comparing the older photographs with the newer ones, noting how you have both changed. Revisit special occasions, exciting vacations, and the beautiful places you've been together. Linger on the faces of friends and loved ones. Read aloud some of the letters you've received from each other, friends, and family. Let your emotions experience again both the angst and the joys you've shared together. Laugh at the outdated clothing and the hairstyles, marvel at the wistful look in your eyes as you gaze out at the world. Remember the anticipated joy you felt then, and rejoice that you found it with each other.

Keep going until you feel a connectedness with the past and a better appreciation for the path along which God has brought you. Remembering can give you a broader point of view, just because it points out how far you've come, how much you've accomplished, how deeply you've loved.

*Recall it often as you wish, a happy memory
never wears out.*
LIBBIE FUDIM

A Moment to Reflect

*I*n scripture, God often instructs his people to remember his commandments and the things he has done for them. In the New Testament, Jesus told his disciples to remember the words he spoke to them, the lessons he taught, the miracles he performed, the events surrounding his life and death. He told them to remember him.

Taking time to remember what God has done for you—the times you've felt his unconditional love, the scrapes he's helped you through, the blessings he's poured out on your lives, can deepen your relationship with him and with each other.

Ah! Memories of sweet summer eves,
Of moonlit wave and willowy way,
Of stars and flowers, and dewy leaves,
And smiles and tones more dear than they!

—JOHN GREENLEAF WHITTIER

The memory of the righteous will be a blessing.
Proverbs 10:7 NIV

A Moment to Refresh

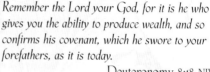

Remember the Lord your God, for it is he who gives you the ability to produce wealth, and so confirms his covenant, which he swore to your forefathers, as it is today.

Deuteronomy 8:18 NIV

He will not often consider the years of his life, because God keeps him occupied with the gladness of his heart.

Ecclesiastes 5:20 NASB

I will call to mind the deeds of the LORD; I will remember your wonders of old.

Psalm 77:11 NRSV

Whenever the rainbow appears in the clouds, I will see it and remember the everlasting covenant between God and all living creatures of every kind on the earth.

Genesis 9:16 NIV

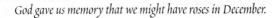

God gave us memory that we might have roses in December.

∾

—*Sir James M. Barrie*

Remember to extol his work, which men have praised in song. All mankind has seen it; men gaze on it from afar.

Job 36:24–25 NIV

Remember His wonderful deeds which He has done, His marvels and the judgments from His mouth.

1 Chronicles 16:12 NASB

Can a woman forget her nursing child, and have no compassion on the son of her womb? Even these may forget, but I will not forget you. Behold, I have inscribed you on the palms of My hands.

Isaiah 49:15–16 NASB

Remember the days of old; consider the generations long past.

Deuteronomy 32:7 NIV

For my part, I travel not to go anywhere, but to go. I travel for travel's sake. The great affair is to move.

∾

—*Robert Louis Stevenson*

Going for a Ride

A Moment to Pause

Climb in your car for a casual getaway for two. Put on your comfortable clothes, don your sunglasses, turn off your cell phone, perhaps pack a few sandwiches and a thermos of coffee.

For this retreat, the fun is in the journey rather than the destination. Have no agenda at all; agree simply that you will head north, south, east, or west, and opt for scenic routes whenever possible. Consider your roadmap as a reference for emergency only. Relax and enjoy the simple things—the hum of the motor, the easy conversation, the good company. Tune in to the sights around you—small towns, interesting buildings, beautiful homes, tranquil country scenes, amusing signs, other motorists.

Focus on the intriguing sounds—the clacking of passing trains, the tooting of factory whistles, the honks from other cars. Luxuriate in the fragrance of blossoming apple trees and wheat fields ready for harvest. Count farmhouses, water towers, out-of-state license plates, cattle, roadside stands.

When you've gone as far as you feel you want to, turn around, change drivers, and head home a different way. By the time you get back, you're apt to feel that even the familiar looks more vibrant and alive.

*We must always have old memories
and young hopes.*
—*Arsene Houssaye*

A Moment to Reflect

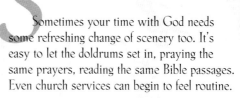

Sometimes your time with God needs some refreshing change of scenery too. It's easy to let the doldrums set in, praying the same prayers, reading the same Bible passages. Even church services can begin to feel routine.

God wants you both to have a living, moving, growing relationship with him. When you start to feel cooped up spiritually, encourage each other to sing him a new song, pray about an issue you haven't prayed about before, read an unfamiliar passage in the Bible, ask questions you haven't asked before. Stir things up. Change the scenery. Take your souls out for a spin

Under this candlelit canopy—
Away from the world's worries—
I felt free to seek new vistas,
Knowing God's light
Always exists,
Even in a world
Of darkness.

—Nanette Thorsen-Snipes

*Go in peace; your way in which you are going
has the LORD's approval.*

Judges 18:6 NASB

A Moment to Refresh

*By day the LORD went ahead of them in a pillar
of cloud to guide them on their way and by night
in a pillar of fire to give them light, so that they
could travel by day or night.*

Exodus 13:21 NIV

*The LORD had said to Abram, "Leave your
country, your people and your father's
household and go to the land I will show you."*

Genesis 12:1 NIV

*The LORD said, "I have come down to deliver
them from the power of the Egyptians, and to
bring them up from that land to a good and
spacious land, to a land flowing with milk and
honey."*

Exodus 3:8 NASB

A person needs at intervals to separate himself from family and companions and go to new places.

—KATHARINE BUTLER HATHAWAY

The LORD your God is bringing you into a good land—a land with streams and pools of water, with springs flowing in the valleys and hills; a land with wheat and barley, vines and fig trees, pomegranates, olive oil and honey; a land where bread will not be scarce and you will lack nothing.

Deuteronomy 8:7–9 NIV

The righteous will inherit the land and dwell in it forever.

Psalm 37:29 NIV

He carried me away in the Spirit to a great and high mountain, and showed me the holy city, Jerusalem, coming down out of heaven from God, having the glory of God. Her brilliance was like a very costly stone.

Revelation 21:10–11 NASB

Change is the watchword of progression. When we tire of well-worn ways, we seek for new.

—ELLA WHEELER WILCOX

Working the Soil

A Moment to Pause

Digging around in the soil is dirty work, but those who have learned to appreciate it will tell you that it's deeply satisfying. Whether the two of you are old hands at gardening or will be trying it for the first time, grab a pair of gloves, find a nice spot, flower pot, or planter, and dig in.

As you work the soil, notice the deep rich colors, the shades of brown, tan, black—even red shows up occasionally. Take a deep breath. Newly turned soil has a wonderful, unique fragrance. Break up the soil with your hands, removing the stones and squeezing the hard clumps with your palms until they crumble and fall away. Now it's time to work the fertilizer into your soil. Dig in together, focusing on seeing that every bit of soil is infused with nutrients.

Finally, it's time to scoop out a place in the soil for your plants—a few or a dozen. Pack the plants in solidly and when you're finished, offer a prayer to God, asking him to bless your plantings with the sunshine and the rain. Then thank him for allowing you to be part of the cycle of life he has created on the earth.

Flowers always make people better, happier and more helpful; they are sunshine, food and medicine to the soul.

—*Luther Burbank*

A Moment to Reflect The Bible uses gardening to illustrate the work God wants to do in the hearts of those who trust him. He is eager to work the soil of your heart as well, breaking up the hard dirt and infusing it with nutrients, and to plant the seeds of everlasting life deep inside where they can grow strong and vital.

God encourages those seeds to grow by pouring the life-giving rains of his grace and the sunshine of his love on your life. Best of all, God's gardening efforts always bring a bountiful harvest of joy, peace, and goodness.

The best things are nearest: breath in your nostrils, light in your eyes, flowers at your feet, duties at your hand, the path of God just before you. Then do not grasp at the stars, but do life's plain, common work as it comes, certain that daily duties and daily bread are the sweetest things of life.

—ROBERT LOUIS STEVENSON

He who gathers in summer is a son who acts wisely.

Proverbs 10:5 NASB

A Moment to Refresh

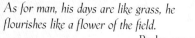

As for man, his days are like grass, he flourishes like a flower of the field.

Psalm 103:15 NIV

The fruit of the Spirit is love, joy, peace, patience, kindness, goodness, faithfulness, gentleness and self-control. Against such things there is no law.

Galatians 5:22–23 NIV

The LORD will make you most prosperous in all the work of your hands and in the fruit of your womb, the young of your livestock and the crops of your land.

Deuteronomy 30:9 NIV

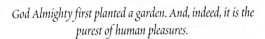

God Almighty first planted a garden. And, indeed, it is the purest of human pleasures.

❧

—FRANCIS BACON

The LORD your God will bless you in all your harvest and in all the work of your hands, and your joy will be complete.
Deuteronomy 16:15 NIV

Jesus said, "I am the true vine, and My Father is the vinedresser. Every branch in Me that does not bear fruit, He takes away; and every branch that bears fruit, He prunes it so that it may bear more fruit."
John 15:1–2 NASB

Behold, the winter is past, the rain is over and gone. The flowers have already appeared in the land; the time has arrived for pruning the vines.
Song of Solomon 2:11–12 NASB

One is nearer God's heart in a garden than anywhere else on earth.

❧

—DOROTHY FRANCES GURNEY

Glorious Slumber

A Moment to Pause Find a comfortable spot and a convenient time to take a sleep retreat. Sleep is an ideal salve. God designed sleep as a natural and necessary element in the cycle of life. Each day you exert yourselves physically, mentally, emotionally and spiritually—and each night you are regenerated in those areas through sleep. Sleep is a ready and available therapy for tension, worry, overwork, and stress.

Begin by turning off the ringer on the phone. Then lie back together, close your eyes, and invite slumber to overtake and envelop you. Nod off to sleep if you can. But if you can't, and if your body and mind seem reluctant to follow your lead and get some rest, there are some things you can do.

Focus your thoughts on God and the wonderful way he has designed your bodies. Starting with your fingers and toes, thank him for each part of your body and for the gift of sleep. Thank God for the day that has passed. Ask him to help you leave the cares and stresses of the day behind and even to help you process them in a way that's helpful as you face tomorrow. Pray for easy, peaceful relaxation.

Sleep is God's celestial nurse who croons away our consciousness, and God deals with the unconscious life of the soul in places where only he and his angels have charge.

—OSWALD CHAMBERS

A Moment to Reflect

God doesn't need to sleep, but he knows that you do. That's the way he designed your body to work. He even set in place a pattern when he created the world in six days and then set aside the seventh for rest. In the Old Testament, this day was called the Sabbath, and it was faithfully enforced.

Seeing that your body, mind, and soul get the regular rest they need by setting aside periods for uninterrupted sleep is now in your hands. It's no longer a law, but it is a principle that continues to benefit those who exercise it.

Sleep is a wonderful thing, but even more wonderful is the morning glory. It is a thrilling thing to wake up and greet a new day with a sense of anticipation. There is a voice that whispers: This is the day! What wonderful and exciting things may happen today.
It is a new day.

—PETER MARSHALL

121

When Jacob awoke from his sleep, he thought,
"Surely the Lord is in this place."

Genesis 28:16 NIV

A Moment to Refresh

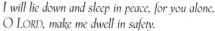

I will lie down and sleep in peace, for you alone,
O LORD, make me dwell in safety.

Psalm 4:8 NIV

When you lie down, you will not be afraid;
when you lie down, your sleep will be sweet.

Proverbs 3:24 NASB

Do this, knowing the time, that it is already the
hour for you to awaken from sleep; for now
salvation is nearer to us than when we believed.

Romans 13:11 NASB

The LORD said, "I will refresh the weary and
satisfy the faint." At this I, Jeremiah, awoke and
looked around. My sleep had been pleasant to
me.

Jeremiah 31:25–26 NIV

I did this night promise my wife never to go to bed without calling upon God, upon my knees, in prayer.

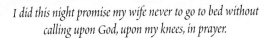

—Samuel Pepys

It is vain for you to rise up early, to retire late, to eat the bread of painful labors; For he gives to His beloved even in his sleep.

Psalm 127:2 NASB

The LORD God caused the man to fall into a deep sleep; and while he was sleeping, he took one of the man's ribs and closed up the place with flesh.

Genesis 2:21 NIV

He will not allow your foot to slip; He who keeps you will not slumber. Behold, He who keeps Israel will neither slumber nor sleep.

Psalm 121:3–4 NASB

I lie down and sleep; I wake again, because the LORD sustains me.

Psalm 3:5 NIV

While others still slept, he went away to pray and to renew his strength in communion with his Father.

—Andrew Murray

Circle of Love

A Moment to Pause The setting for this retreat can be anywhere you feel comfortable. Indoors or outdoors, both are good. The goal is simply to focus together on God, the one who created you to love and be loved. God loves you—both of you—deeply and constantly. The Bible compares his love to a river, so deep you can be submerged in it. Take a few moments to step down into the water and experience God's love together in a very special way.

Hold hands with each other and lift your free hands to heaven. Imagine that God is taking both your hands and completing your circle of love. Then open your hearts to receive all that he wishes to give you as children of a loving and benevolent father.

You will need no guidance for what happens next, for it will be as new, as unexpected, as unique as God himself. Simply respond in whatever way seems right to you—sing, laugh, weep, jump, dance, kneel before him. Your hearts will know what to do. Leap into the river. Let it surround you, lift you, cleanse you. In that place, you will find all things good and honorable and lasting.

In this is love, not that we loved God but that he
loved us and send his Son to be the atoning
sacrifice for our sins.
1 JOHN 4:10 NRSV

A Moment to Reflect

God's love is a gift. It cannot be earned. It cannot be bought for any price. It is freely available, and it can only be received, experienced, and responded to. The human frame was just not strong enough to reach to heaven, so God reached to earth, pouring out his love on all those who choose to reach back.

Choose today to make God a part of your circle of love. Let him immerse your hearts and teach you what true love is really about. Experiencing God's love is a retreat for the soul that will change your lives forever.

O Love that will not let me go,
I rest my weary soul in thee,
I give thee back the life I owe,
That in thine ocean depths its flow
May richer, fuller, be.

—George Matheson

Having loved his own who were in the world,
he now showed them the full extent of his love.

John 13:1 NIV

A Moment to Refresh

Remain in me, and I will remain in you. No
branch can bear fruit by itself; it must remain in
the vine.

John 15:4 NIV

Christ's love compels us, because we are
convinced that one died for all, and therefore
all died.

2 Corinthians 5:14 NIV

Your lovingkindness is great above the heavens;
and Your truth reaches to the skies.

Psalm 108:4 NASB

How priceless is your unfailing love! Both high
and low among men find refuge in the shadow of
your wings.

Psalm 36:7 NIV

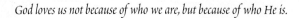

God loves us not because of who we are, but because of who He is.

—AUTHOR UNKNOWN

The LORD's lovingkindnesses indeed never cease, for His compassions never fail.
Lamentations 3:22 NASB

The steadfast love of the LORD is from everlasting to everlasting on those who fear him.
Psalm 103:17 NRSV

The LORD your God is God; he is the faithful God, keeping his covenant of love to a thousand generations of those who love him and keep his commands.
Deuteronomy 7:9 NIV

I trust in God's unfailing love for ever and ever.
Psalm 52:8 NIV

All God can give us is his love; and this love becomes tangible—a burning of the soul—it sets us on fire to the point of forgetting ourselves.

– BROTHER ROGER

At Inspirio we love to hear from you—your
stories, your feedback,
and your product ideas.
Please send your comments to us
by way of e-mail at
icares@zondervan.com
or to the address below:

Ψ

inspirio

Attn: Inspirio Cares
5300 Patterson Avenue SE
Grand Rapids, MI 49530

If you would like further information
about Inspirio and the products we
create please visit us at:
www.inspiriogifts.com

Thank you and God Bless!